World of Science

Adventures with Germs and Your Health

Written by
Benedict Boo

Illustrated by
Alan Bay

WS Education

NEW JERSEY • LONDON • SINGAPORE • BEIJING • SHANGHAI • HONG KONG • TAIPEI • CHENNAI • TOKYO

Published by

WS Education, an imprint of
World Scientific Publishing Co. Pte. Ltd.
5 Toh Tuck Link, Singapore 596224
USA office: 27 Warren Street, Suite 401-402, Hackensack, NJ 07601
UK office: 57 Shelton Street, Covent Garden, London WC2H 9HE

National Library Board, Singapore Cataloguing in Publication Data
Name(s): Boo, Benedict. | Bay, Alan, illustrator.
Title: Adventures with germs and your health / written by Benedict Boo; illustrated by Alan Bay.
Other Title(s): World of science ; 12.
Description: Singapore : WS Education, [2022]
Identifier(s): ISBN 978-981-12-5448-2 (hardcover) | 978-981-12-5449-9 (paperback) |
978-981-12-5450-5 (ebook for institutions) | 978-981-12-5451-2 (ebook for individuals)
Subject(s): LCSH: Bacteria--Comic books, strips, etc. | Bacteria--Juvenile literature. |
Microorganisms--Comic books, strips, etc. | Microorganisms--Juvenile literature. |
Health--Comic books, strips, etc. | Health--Juvenile literature. | Graphic novels.
Classification: DDC 579.3--dc23

British Library Cataloguing-in-Publication Data
A catalogue record for this book is available from the British Library.

Design and layout: Loo Chuan Ming

Printed in Singapore

What are germs?

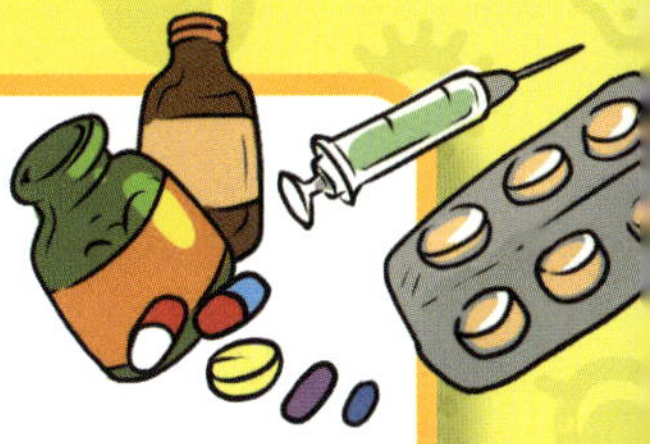

They are all around us, on us and even inside us, but how much do we know about germs? So tiny that they are invisible to the naked eye, the four main types of germs outnumber all visible species on Earth!

What's the difference between a cold and the flu? Why should you get vaxxed against COVID-19? Grow your good bacteria, fight cancer and bust some common myths about diseases! Get up close and personal with the microscopic living things that hold the key to good health.

Experience a world of interactive discoveries!

Scan to watch a video on activating AR in 3 easy steps.

1

Download the SnapLearn app.

2

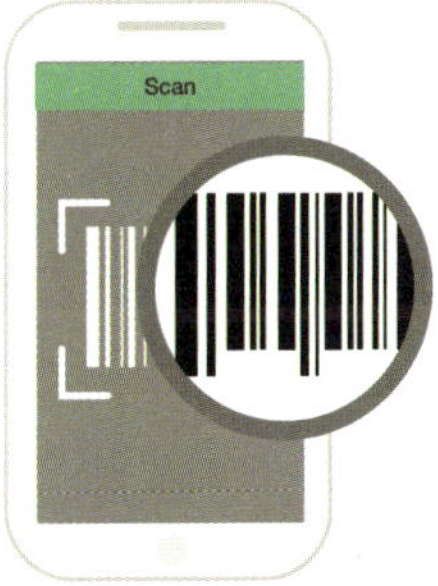

Activate by scanning this book's barcode. Then, tap on the book cover image on your screen.

3

Wherever you see this icon, scan the whole page.

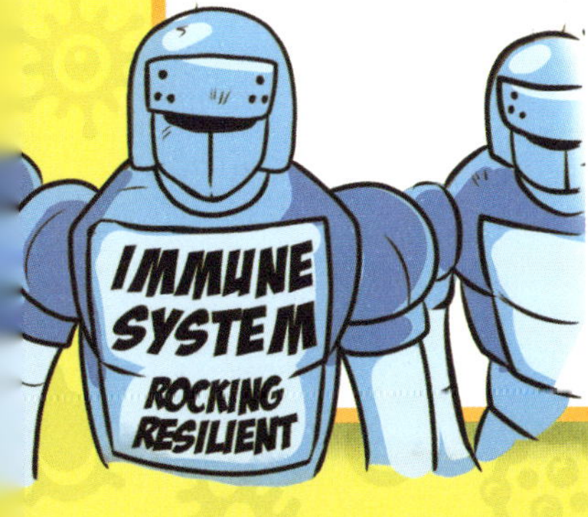

Contents

ALL ABOUT GERMS

DREADFUL DISEASES

World of Germs

Germ Profiles

Viruses cannot store or make energy on their own. They need the cells of other organisms in order to survive and reproduce. Bacteria are tiny single-celled creatures that can reproduce on their own. Fungi are multi-celled and absorb their food from their surroundings. Like bacteria, protozoa are single-celled. They feed on organic matter, including other microorganisms, and often travel in contaminated water.

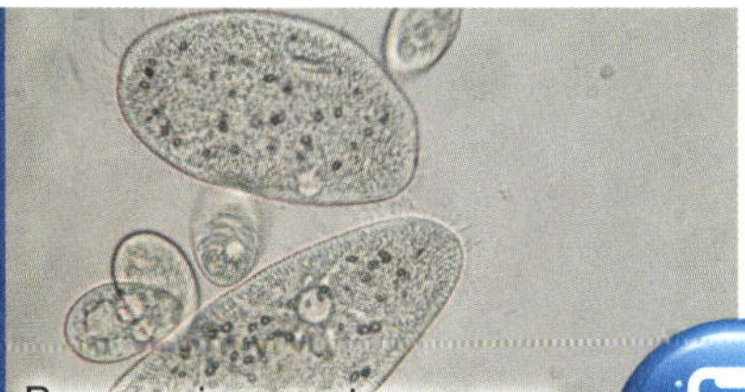

Paramecium protozoa seen through a microscope

Brush Up!

Did you know that around 700 species of bacteria live in your mouth? They feed on sugars from the food and drinks you consume, producing acids that can cause tooth decay. Regularly brushing your teeth removes food particles and freshens your breath. In addition, many kinds of toothpaste contain ingredients that protect your teeth and gums from harmful bacteria.

Gut Feelings

Probiotics are live bacteria (right) and yeasts that help keep the digestive system healthy. Prebiotics are types of fibre that feed the good bacteria in the digestive system.

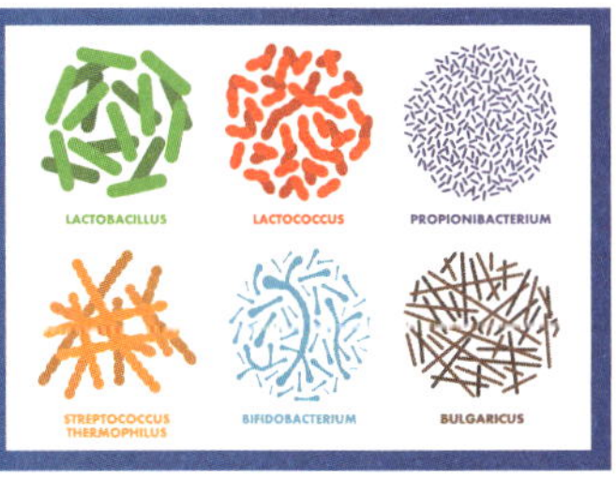

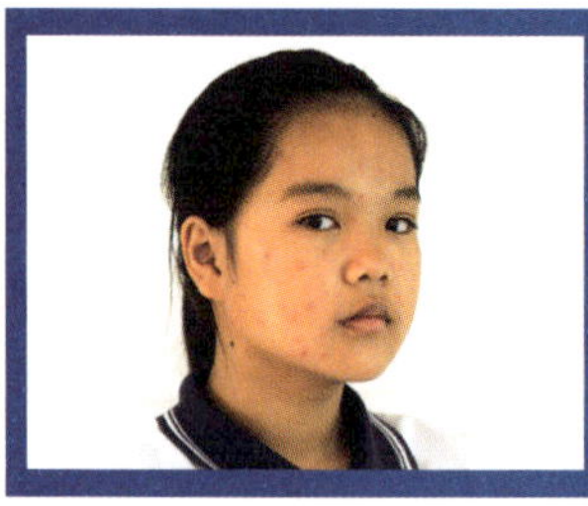

What Are These Red Spots?

Chickenpox is a very contagious disease caused by the herpes zoster virus. Symptoms include a fever and itchy red blisters on the hands, legs and body. Chickenpox is usually mild in healthy children, but in severe cases, blisters may also form on the face and scalp.

What's Growing on My Toes?

Athlete's foot is also known as tinea pedis. It is a common fungal infection that can occur under warm, damp conditions, such as when feet are sweaty, not dried after swimming or bathing, or confined in tight-fitting socks or shoes. Fungal growth usually starts between the toes and spreads, becoming an itchy, stinging or burning rash.

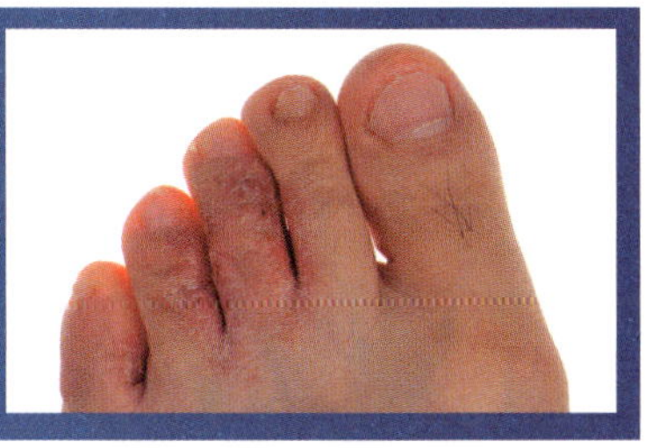

Good Bacteria Gives Us Gut Health!

How does good bacteria keep our digestive system healthy?

Each person has a microbiome, a world of microorganisms, including bacteria, fungi, parasites and viruses, concentrated in the small and large intestines.

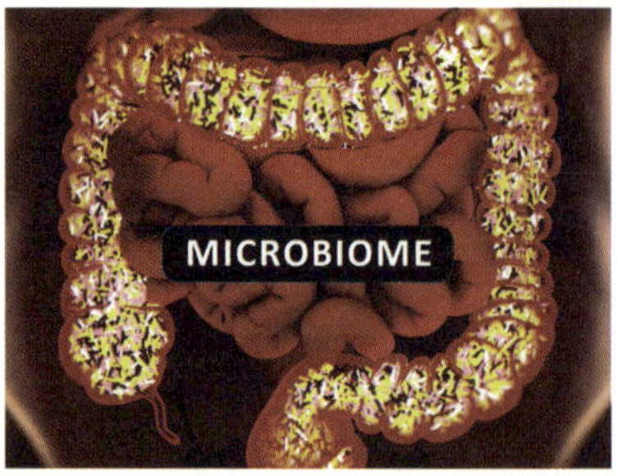

In a healthy body, good and bad bacteria live together in balance within the microbiome. However, illness or a course of antibiotics can disrupt the balance.

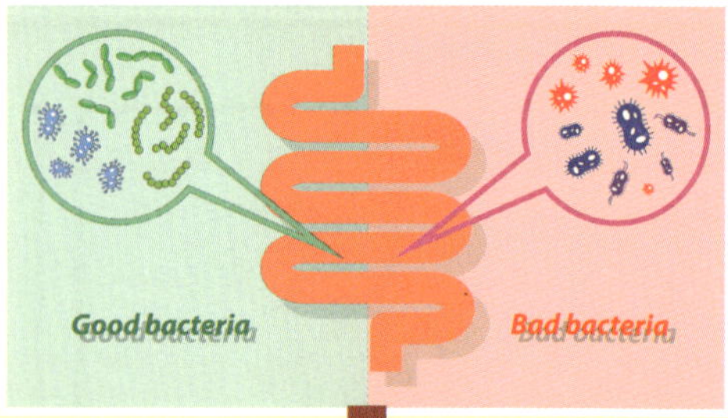

We can regain good gut bacteria by eating probiotics, which are live bacteria and yeasts present in yoghurt, sauerkraut, kimchi, tempeh and other fermented foods.

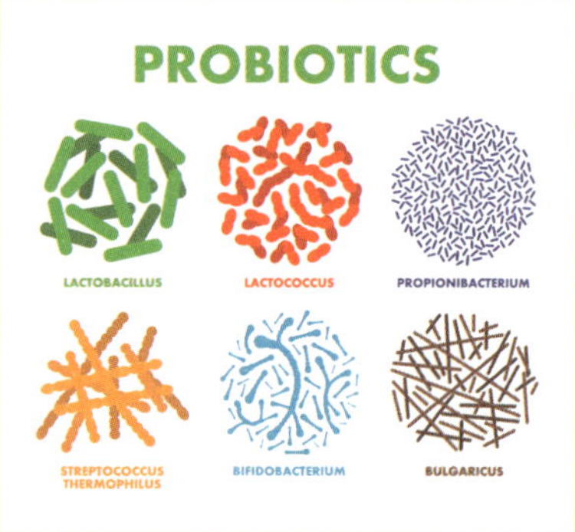

Prebiotics are natural substances in some foods that encourage the growth of healthy bacteria in the gut.

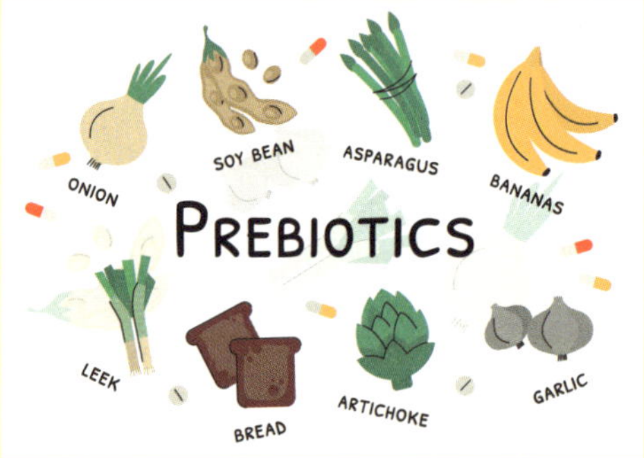

A healthy gut affects more than just the digestive system. It is believed to improve overall physical and mental health.

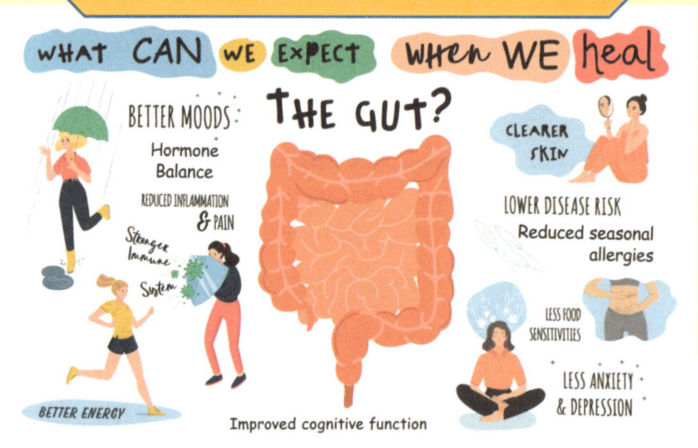

Hidden Fortress

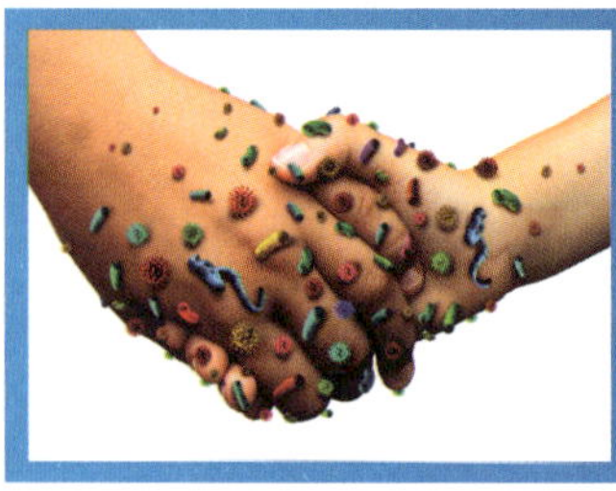

How Germs Travel

Our bodies are surrounded by and exposed to germs all the time. Harmful germs, also known as pathogens, can spread through the air when an infected person coughs or sneezes. They can also travel in body fluids such as blood, saliva or sweat. Pathogens can also be spread through physical contact, such as by shaking hands with an infected person and then touching your eyes, nose or mouth.

Ditch the Damp and Dirty

Germs do well in warm, protein-rich environments, such as in bins where there is decaying food or organic waste. Keeping our bodies and living environment clean and dry is a good way to prevent the growth and spread of disease-causing germs.

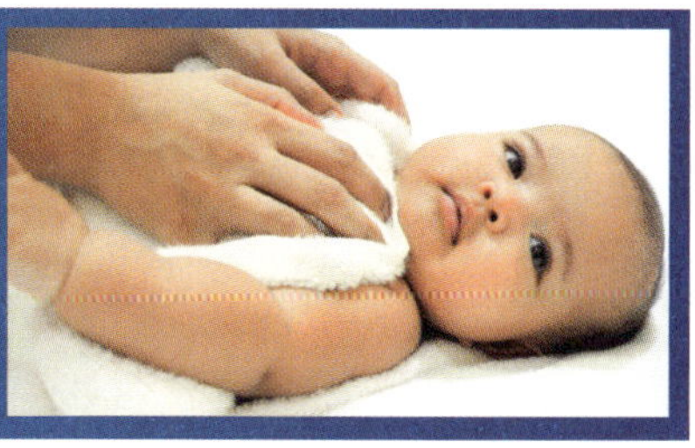

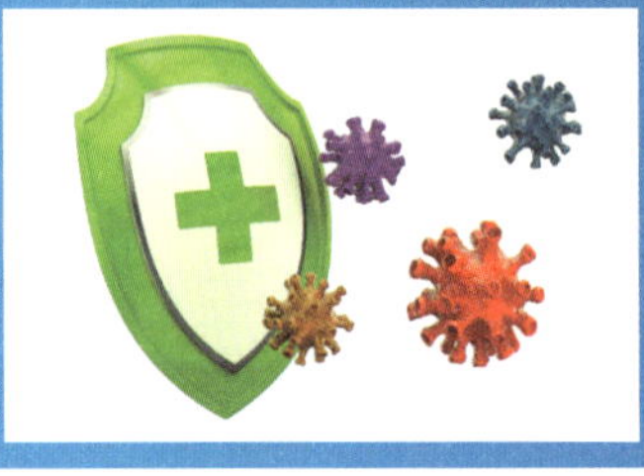

Lines of Defence

When pathogens enter the human body, the tissues, cells and proteins of the immune system work together to defend the body. The body's cells either capture and eliminate the pathogens directly, or produce proteins known as antibodies to destroy the pathogens. Find out more on the next page!

Amazing Immune System

Did you know that your body's immune system is made up of special units that deal with harmful germs as a team?

Pathogens that invade the body produce proteins known as antigens. In this illustration (left), antigens are represented as spikes on the surface of a cell that has been infected by a virus.

Human blood consists of red blood cells, white blood cells, platelets and plasma. Around 20–40 percent of our white blood cells are lymphocytes. Lymphocytes circulate in the blood. Their role is to detect antigens.

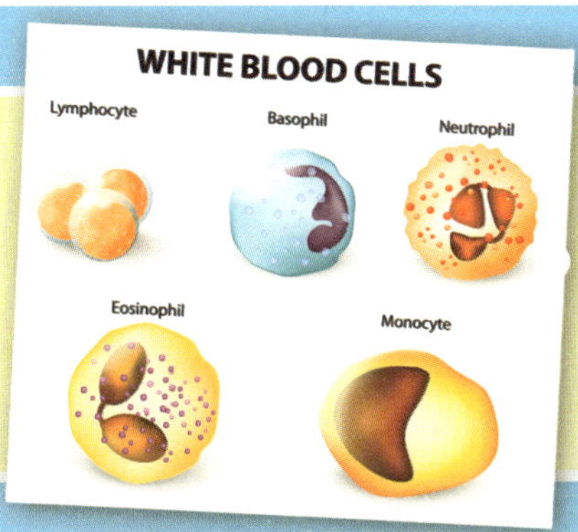

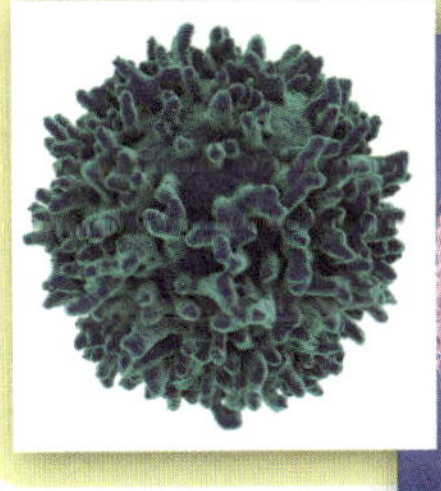

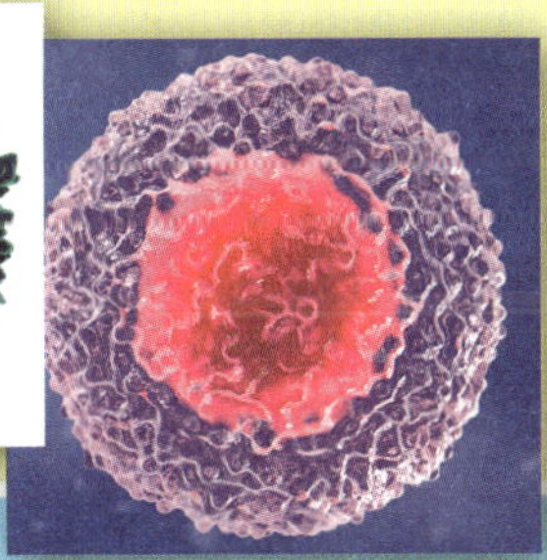

Our bone marrow produces two types of lymphocytes: B-lymphocytes and T-lymphocytes. A B-lymphocyte (far left) produces antibodies that attach themselves to antigens and disable them. It may also "tag" antigens for other cells to destroy. A T-lymphocyte (left) attacks and destroys the antigens as well as infected cells.

Antibodies are Y-shaped proteins produced by B-lymphocytes in response to antigens. After recovering from an infection or receiving a vaccine, a number of antibodies remain in your system, together with antibody-producing B-lymphocytes. When your body next encounters the same type of germ, your B-lymphocytes "remember" the enemy. Immune response is much faster, and you are better able to fight off infection.

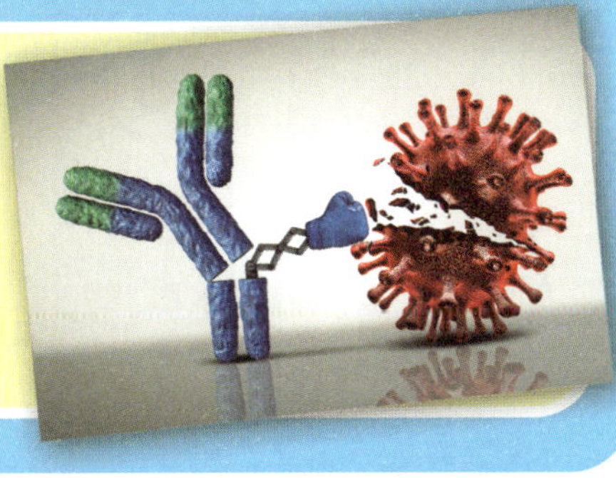

In Fact... Or Not?

What's the Difference?

We often confuse the common cold with influenza, also known as the flu. Both are contagious diseases that affect the respiratory (breathing) system, but they are caused by different kinds of viruses. Turn to page 52 to find out more about the common cold!

SYMPTOMS	FEVER	HEADACHE	ACHES	FATIGUE, WEAKNESS	STUFFY OR RUNNY NOSE	SNEEZING	SORE THROAT	COUGH
COLD	RARE	RARE	SLIGHT	MILD	COMMON	USUAL	COMMON	MILD TO MODERATE
FLU	HIGH, CAN LAST 3-4 DAYS	COMMON	COMMON, CAN BE SEVERE	INTENSE, CAN LAST A FEW WEEKS	SOMETIMES	SOMETIMES	SOMETIMES	COMMON, CAN BECOME SEVERE

Disease	Incubation period
Influenza	1–3 days
Dengue fever	3–14 days
Chickenpox	9–21 days
Measles	9–12 days
COVID-19	2–14 days

How Long?

The incubation period of an infectious disease is the time between exposure to it and the appearance of the first signs or symptoms. The table (left) shows the incubation periods of some common viruses.

No Connection

Germs require a medium to travel from an infected person to a new host. They can travel through the air when someone coughs or sneezes, through liquids (such as blood or saliva) or through direct contact. But they cannot spread through a phone or video call.

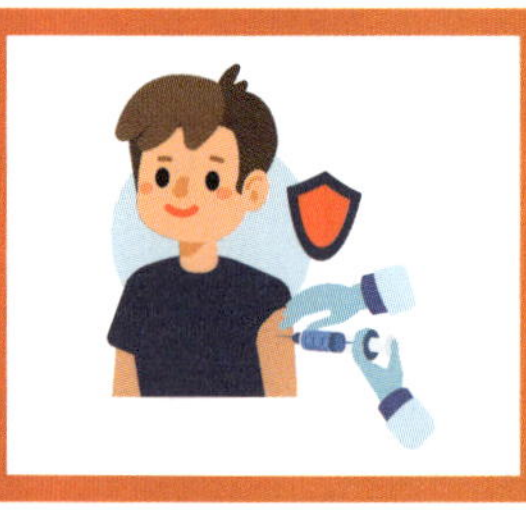

Vaccines Protect, Not Infect

Flu vaccines are made with viruses that have already been killed, so they cannot cause a vaccinated person to get the flu. The nasal spray flu vaccine does use a weakened live flu virus, but this has been modified so that it survives only in the nose. It is unable to reproduce in warmer parts of the body, such as the lungs.

Superstitions and False Beliefs

Throughout history, there have been many myths about how diseases spread. For example, during the 3rd century, people believed that the Plague of Cyprian could be caught by looking at the face of an infected person. In the mid-14th century, when the Black Death killed more than 20 million people in Europe, many believed that the plague was caused by the movement of planets.

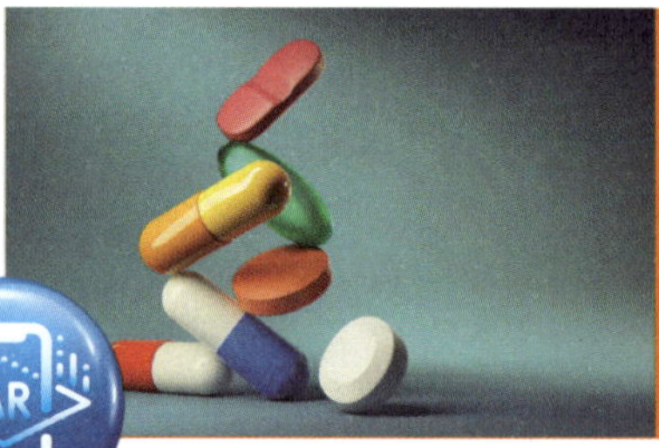

Antibiotic Resistance

Antibiotics work by killing bacteria, but they are not effective against viral infections and should not be taken for the flu. The bacteria in our bodies can develop resistance to frequently used antibiotics. If this happens, antibiotic treatment may fail when we really need it to fight serious bacterial infections.

Get It?

Not all diseases are infectious. You cannot catch diseases such as diabetes, epilepsy, Alzheimer's disease or cancer from an infected person. Noninfectious diseases are usually caused by factors such as diet, genetics, lifestyle or environment.

Cancer Contingents

Well, my heroes aren't germs, but they sure are strong!
Ah, he's talking about cancer-causing agents! They're here too!
Yes, they're our finest forces, the Carcinogen Contingents!
Car-ci... what? Are they the ones in the big tanks?
No. They are the best, but they are not the largest. In fact, they are quite tiny. That helps them hide and move around faster.
I know, are they those stealthy ones over there?
Yes, you spotted them! Do you know how deadly they are?

Let me guess… Have they killed more than 1 million humans?
10,000,000
Way more than that. In a recent year, they killed about 10 million people!
That's amazing! What's their secret?
Well, their strategy is to enter the human body and damage some of its cells.
That doesn't sound very deadly… Is that all?
These damaged cells grow abnormally. Unlike healthy cells, which reach a resting phase and die, abnormal cells keep on making copies of themselves. Eventually, they form a tumour.

Still doesn't sound dangerous to me.
Be patient. Some tumours are nonthreatening. But cancerous tumours grow into nearby tissues. As they get oxygen and nutrients from nearby blood vessels, cancer cells can break off…
Benign Tumour
Malignant Tumour
I've heard of that happening! Such tumours are malignant, meaning that they can metastasise, or spread to other parts of the body.
That's right, and cancer cells can spread very quickly to the lymph nodes and other parts of the body, once they break off from a malignant tumour and enter the blood vessels.
I see. Malignant tumours then form in other parts of the body too, eventually invading organs and tissues, and causing death.
Wow. Carcinogens may be small, but they sure can cause huge damage in the end!
Don't be fooled by their humble appearance!

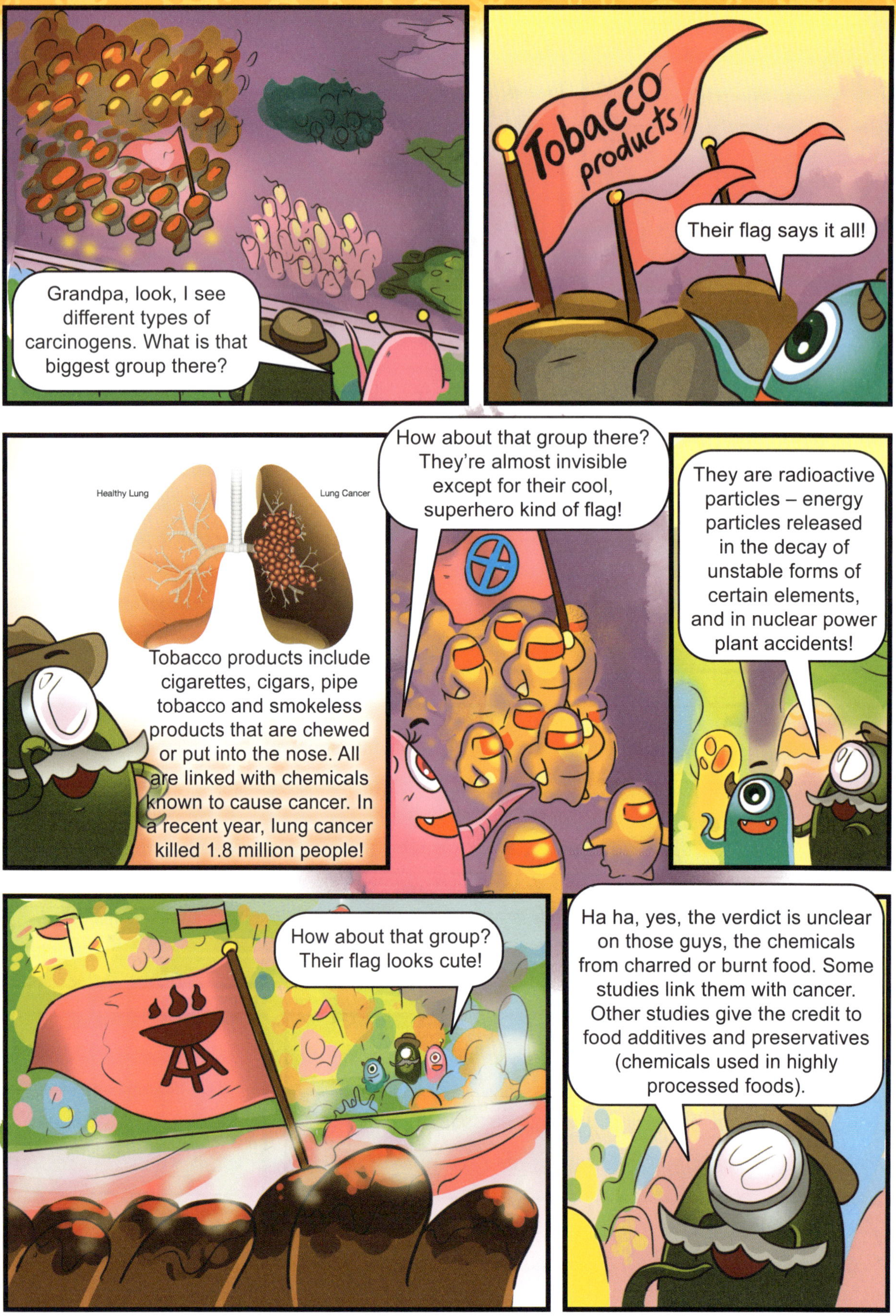
Grandpa, look, I see different types of carcinogens. What is that biggest group there?
Tobacco products
Their flag says it all!
Healthy Lung
Lung Cancer
Tobacco products include cigarettes, cigars, pipe tobacco and smokeless products that are chewed or put into the nose. All are linked with chemicals known to cause cancer. In a recent year, lung cancer killed 1.8 million people!
How about that group there? They're almost invisible except for their cool, superhero kind of flag!
They are radioactive particles – energy particles released in the decay of unstable forms of certain elements, and in nuclear power plant accidents!
How about that group? Their flag looks cute!
Ha ha, yes, the verdict is unclear on those guys, the chemicals from charred or burnt food. Some studies link them with cancer. Other studies give the credit to food additives and preservatives (chemicals used in highly processed foods).

Whether or not burnt food causes cancer, humans who eat a lot of it are probably eating fewer healthy foods, so it's a win-win situation for us!
On a more serious note, it's not enough to know only about our troops. We need to understand our enemy as well.
IMMUNE SYSTEM
ROCKING
Do you mean the human body's natural defences?
Yes, their immune systems get stronger with a healthy, balanced diet, enough rest and sleep, and physical exercise.
Thanks for teaching us so much about our forces and our enemies, Grandpa. I feel like I'm all ready for battle now!
You're still young. Let's just enjoy the parade for now!

What Is Cancer?

Cancer is a disease caused when cells in the body divide uncontrollably, spreading into surrounding tissues. Cancer can be caused by genetic factors, pathogens or carcinogens, toxic chemicals that damage the cells' DNA (deoxyribonucleic acid, the material containing information for how the cell should grow to build and maintain the body). Abnormal cells grow, divide and spread in ways that harm the body.

Radioactive waste is a carcinogen.

Abnormal cells reproduce quickly, forming a tumour (a lump of cells). It can be benign (nonthreatening) or malignant.

Benign tumours grow slowly, usually remaining where they are.

Malignant tumours grow rapidly. Cancer cells from them may enter blood vessels.

Malignant tumours invade surrounding tissues, destroying them.

They metastasise, forming new tumours in other parts of the body.

METASTASES

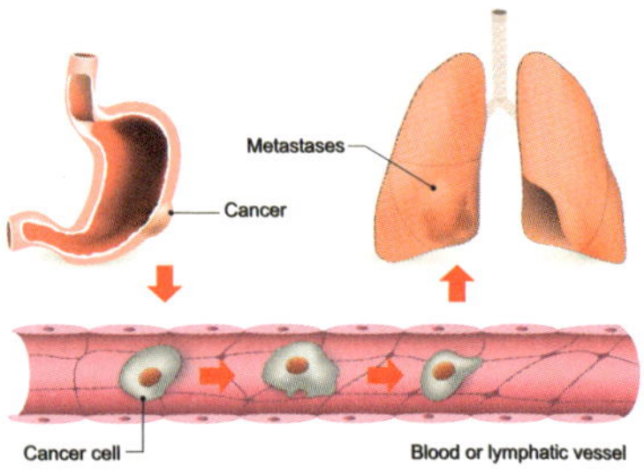

Important notes:
(i) Carcinogens are toxic substances but they are not considered germs.
(ii) About 20 percent of all known cancers are caused by pathogens. For instance, the hepatitis B and C viruses are strongly linked to liver cancer.

A Serious Coronavirus

Can Pets Spread COVID-19?

Some pet owners are worried about infecting their pets with COVID-19 or catching the disease from infected pets. Although there have been news reports of some animals falling sick with COVID-19, there is no conclusive evidence that the virus can be transmitted from pets to humans.

Keep a Safe Distance

Like other viruses, COVID-19 is spread through droplets and particles released into the air by an infected person. Larger droplets fall to the ground, but smaller particles may stay in the air, landing on or being breathed in by others. Therefore mask wearing, social distancing and hand washing are effective means of slowing the spread of the virus.

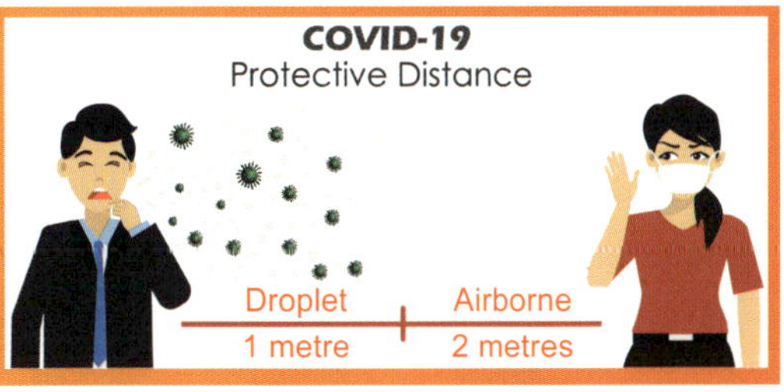

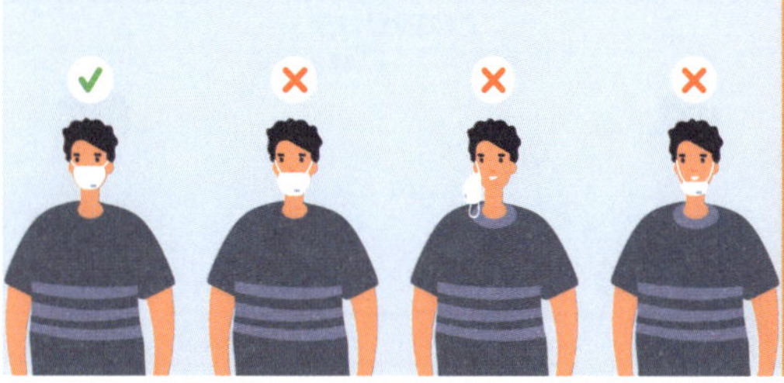

Mask Up!

Mask wearing does not make it impossible for a person to catch COVID-19, but it significantly reduces the chances. Clean your hands before putting on and after taking off your mask. Ensure that your mask fits snugly, covering all of your nose and mouth. When removing your mask temporarily (for example to eat or drink), store it in a clean bag.

A Family of Coronaviruses

Severe acute respiratory syndrome (SARS) is a viral respiratory disease caused by a SARS coronavirus. It was first identified in 2003. In 2012, another coronavirus emerged, in Saudi Arabia. Middle East respiratory syndrome coronavirus (MERS-CoV) infects humans and dromedary camels. The coronavirus that causes COVID-19 (coronavirus disease 2019) is officially called Severe acute respiratory syndrome coronavirus 2 (SARS-CoV-2). It was discovered in 2019.

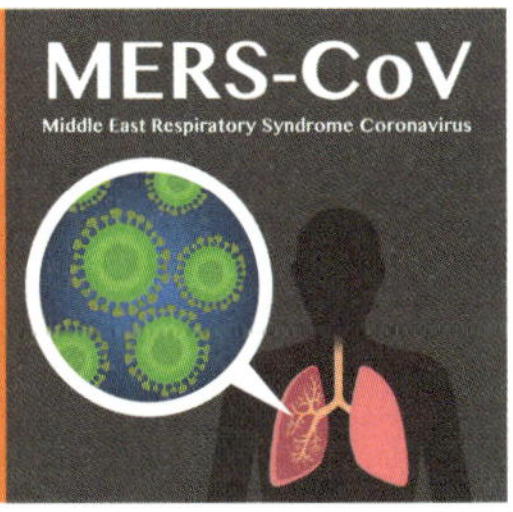

COVID-19 Virus Structure

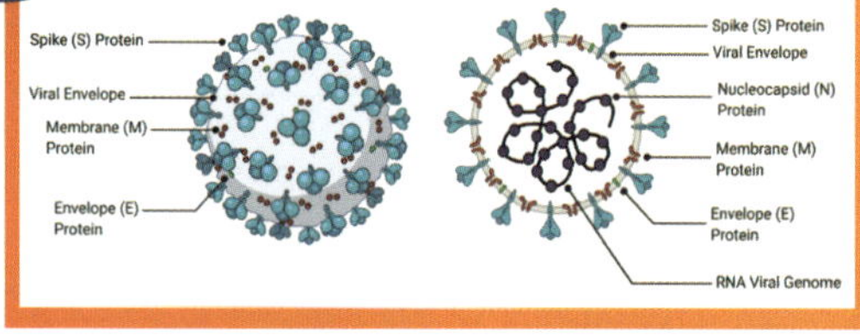

Keeping an Eye on Variants

The COVID-19 virus has a distinct spike protein structure made up of 1,273 amino acids. Each particle surface has about 26 spike trimers (a group of three spike proteins). Some mutations to the spike proteins allow the virus to spread more easily or make it resistant to treatments or vaccines. Those variants must be monitored more carefully.

Stay Home, Stay Safe

A lockdown is a policy of restricting the movement of people during times when open interaction is risky, such as during war or the outbreak of infectious diseases. Staying at home helps stop community-wide spread of coronaviruses by limiting human contact.

Get Vaxxed!

It's so good to be back at the beach again! Do you remember what happened the last time we came?
Yes, Jayden! We built that super cool sandcastle, just for Otis!
Hey, let's try something different this time. Remember what we saw in that magazine?

Yes! Let's try the sand-sational treatment for King Otis!
What's wrong, Tammy? You look worried.
I've been thinking about my mum and her vaccination appointment next week. She's afraid that the jab will hurt…
AR
My dad said the needle was long and sharp… Yikes!
Tsk, don't listen to Jayden!
Yeah, don't worry, Mum will be fine. Come, let's go for a swim!

Oh dear, I think Otis is afraid of swimming in the sea!
Come in, Otie boy, it's okay. Look, we're all here!
I have an idea!

Wow, that was really smart of you, Jayden!
Thank Tammy. She gave me the idea.

Huh? What did I do?
Tammy only mentioned vaccination… You didn't give Otis a jab, did you?
No, I didn't! Don't you know how vaccines work?
Hmm… all I know is that vaccines protect us from viruses. But how do they actually work, Jayden?
Some vaccines teach our cells how to make a protein, triggering an immune response in our bodies. Other vaccines actually contain the virus we are protecting ourselves from!
AR
What??? Wouldn't those vaccines infect us?
VIRUS
KILLED VIRUS
(virus is killed or modified in such a way that it is unable to replicate)
ANTIBODIES
(target a specific pathogen)
No, because they contain only a weakened or inactivated version of the virus.

When we receive these versions of the virus, our body learns to produce the antibodies that fight the virus.
Oh, I get it now! You introduced Otis to the small pool, so that he could learn to cope with getting a little wet first. Then he could deal with jumping into the sea!
Smart! But why is Mum's COVID-19 vaccination split up into two doses?
The first dose of the vaccine starts the process of building up protection. But it produces a relatively weak immune response. The second dose works to greatly reinforce this protection. Booster shots may be needed later, to increase antibody levels that decline after some time.
That sounds a bit like learning a new basketball skill this week, letting it sink into our muscle memory, then practising it again next week to make sure we have learnt it well.
I see! Understanding how vaccines work definitely helps us overcome our fear of them! When we get home, I'll tell Mum all about this, in case she doesn't know yet.
Great! If Otis can conquer his fears, your mum can do it too!

Load Up on Ammo!

The paintball instructor briefs the team…
A while later…
Psssst psssst...
Mike, our opponents look strong.
They'll be saying the same thing about us! I'm sure we can <croak> beat them!
PHHHWEEEEEEETTT!!!
That's the whistle. Let's start!!

Where are all our bullets?
Let's tell the staff!
No time for that! Just run and try your best to avoid getting hit!

That wasn't fair! We had no ammunition.
Yes, there was no way we could fight like that!
Dad was the one who told them to take away all our ammunition.
WHY???

We wanted you to understand what it is like to go without medication when you are ill.
Yes, it is just like going into a paintball match with no ammunition.
Medicines perform many important functions for us. They are essential for our recovery and wellbeing.
Oh, I see. Now I'll remember to take my medicine when I need to.
Mum, Dad, I promise to take my sore throat medication the moment we get home. But now may we play one more match, please? With ammunition this time?

Medication in Our Bodies

Did you know that medicines work in several different ways?

Busting Bacteria

Antibiotics help destroy or slow the growth of bacteria in bacterial infections. For example, penicillin is an effective treatment for ear, mouth and throat infections.

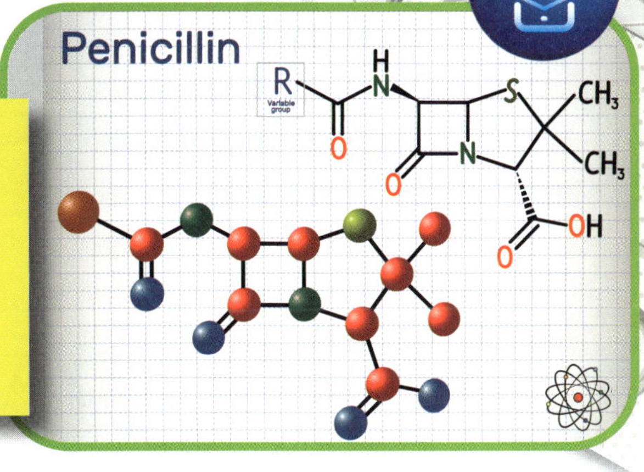

Relieving Pain

Medicines can also soothe discomfort or pain from illness or injury. For example, ibuprofen (isobutylphenyl propionic acid) is a painkiller that relieves fever and reduces soreness and swelling. It is used to treat muscular strains and arthritis, a painful condition in which the joints of the body become swollen.

Boosting Chemicals

Medication helps when our bodies are unable to produce sufficient quantities of certain chemicals or substances. For example, people with diabetes cannot produce enough insulin, the chemical that controls blood sugar levels. Insulin injections can replace or supplement the body's insulin production.

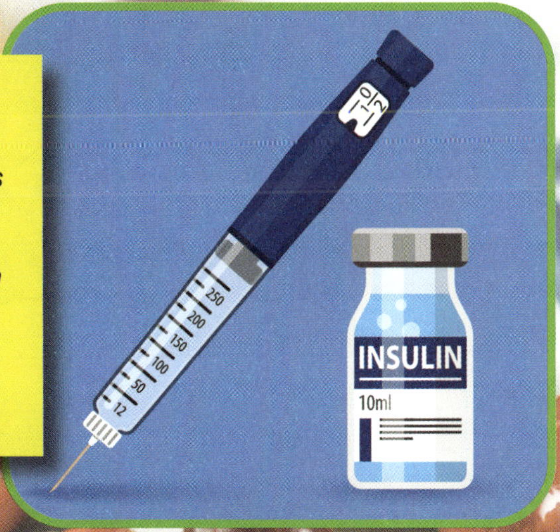

What's So Common About Your Cold?

Ahh Chooo!

The common cold is the most frequently suffered infectious human disease in the world. It is an infection of the upper respiratory system (the breathing system that includes the nose and throat). More than 200 viruses can cause a cold. Many of them belong to a group called rhinoviruses, whose name comes from a Greek word meaning "nose".

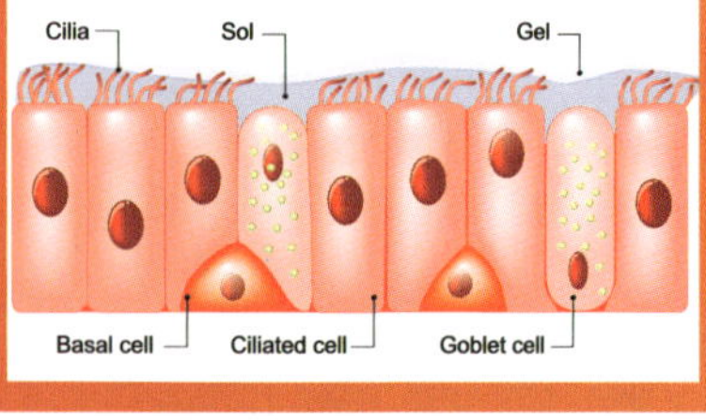

What's in a Sneeze or Cough?

Mucus is made up of sticky proteins called mucins, and other proteins that kill or disable germs. Our noses and throats are lined with goblet cells and ciliated cells. When we catch a cold, goblet cells produce more mucus to trap pathogens. Ciliated cells are covered with tiny hairlike structures that clear the mucus from our airways. Extra mucus triggers coughing, which expels pathogens and mucus from our bodies.

Don't Spread a Cold!

When an infected person sneezes or coughs, pathogens are released into the surrounding air. Virus particles can travel up to 4 metres and survive for a few hours outside the body. If they are inhaled, they can infect another person. That's why it's a good idea to wear a mask or minimise contact with other people when we have a cold.

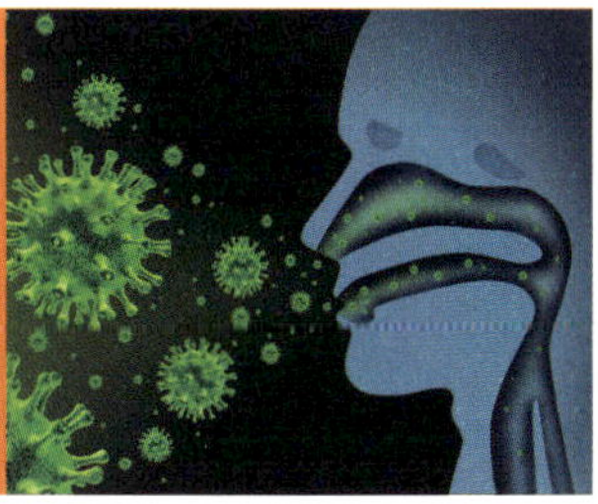

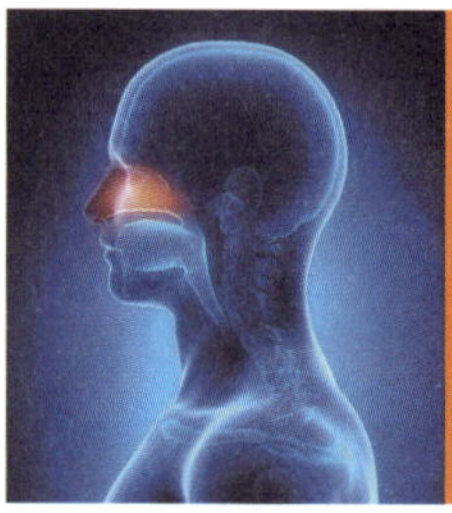

Why Is My Nose Blocked?

Nasal congestion, also known as a blocked or stuffy nose, can be caused by several different conditions, including viral and bacterial infections, allergies and pollutants such as vehicle exhaust fumes or tobacco smoke. These can trigger swelling or inflammation of the nasal membranes (tissues in the nose), resulting in nasal congestion.

An Interconnected System

The ear, nose and throat are considered part of the same system because they are closely connected by canals and pathways known as the mucous membranes. This means that bacteria or viruses can easily travel from an infected ear, nose or throat to the other parts of the system. A doctor who specialises in ENT conditions is known as an otolaryngologist.

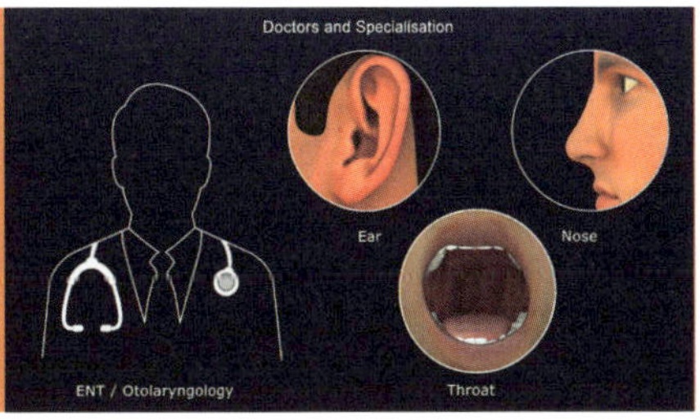

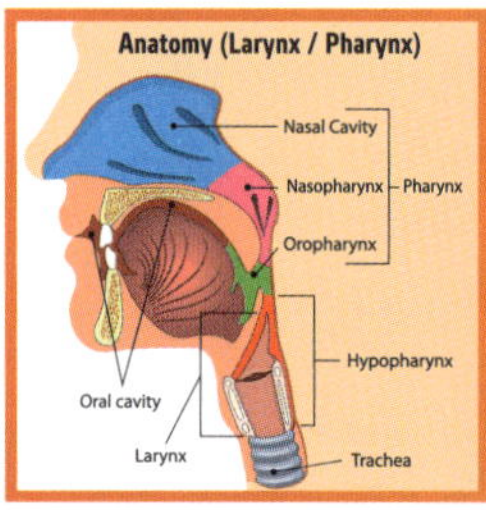

Signs of a Cold

Cold symptoms can vary, depending on which part of the respiratory system is infected. A stuffy or runny nose indicates that the nasal cavity is infected. An infection of the larynx results in coughing or loss of voice. A sore throat indicates an infection of the pharynx. A fever results when the body raises its temperature to try to kill off pathogens.

Get Well Soon!

What are the best remedies for a cold? Rest recharges the body's immune system. Drinking plenty of water helps us stay hydrated and relieves nasal congestion. Medication helps manage cold symptoms. For example, an antihistamine can stop a runny nose for a time; decongestants can relieve a cough; painkillers or a saltwater gargle can soothe a sore throat.

Throwing Up or Passing Out?

We have been using that strategy for the last 6 months, and look at our results!
That's because humans have learnt how to deal with it.
Yes, they learn fast. What do you suggest, Sniper?
I say we develop special viruses. Target specific individuals and kill everyone who gets infected.
That's effective, but it would take too long. Does anyone have a better idea?
Sir, we need to think smart. Smarter than them.
Don't get smart with me, soldier. Just tell me what your plan is!
Yes, sir! I say we attack them where they are weak!

They are weak in their… legs?
I think they're weak in their hearts!
No. Here is their weakness!
You're right! That's brilliant! Humans can't resist eating. That's how we'll get them!
As my hero Sun Tzu, the Chinese general and military theorist, once said, "If you know the enemy and know yourself, you need not fear the result of a hundred battles."
Alright, let's do this! Go find out how we can use their bottomless appetites against them!
Yes, sir!

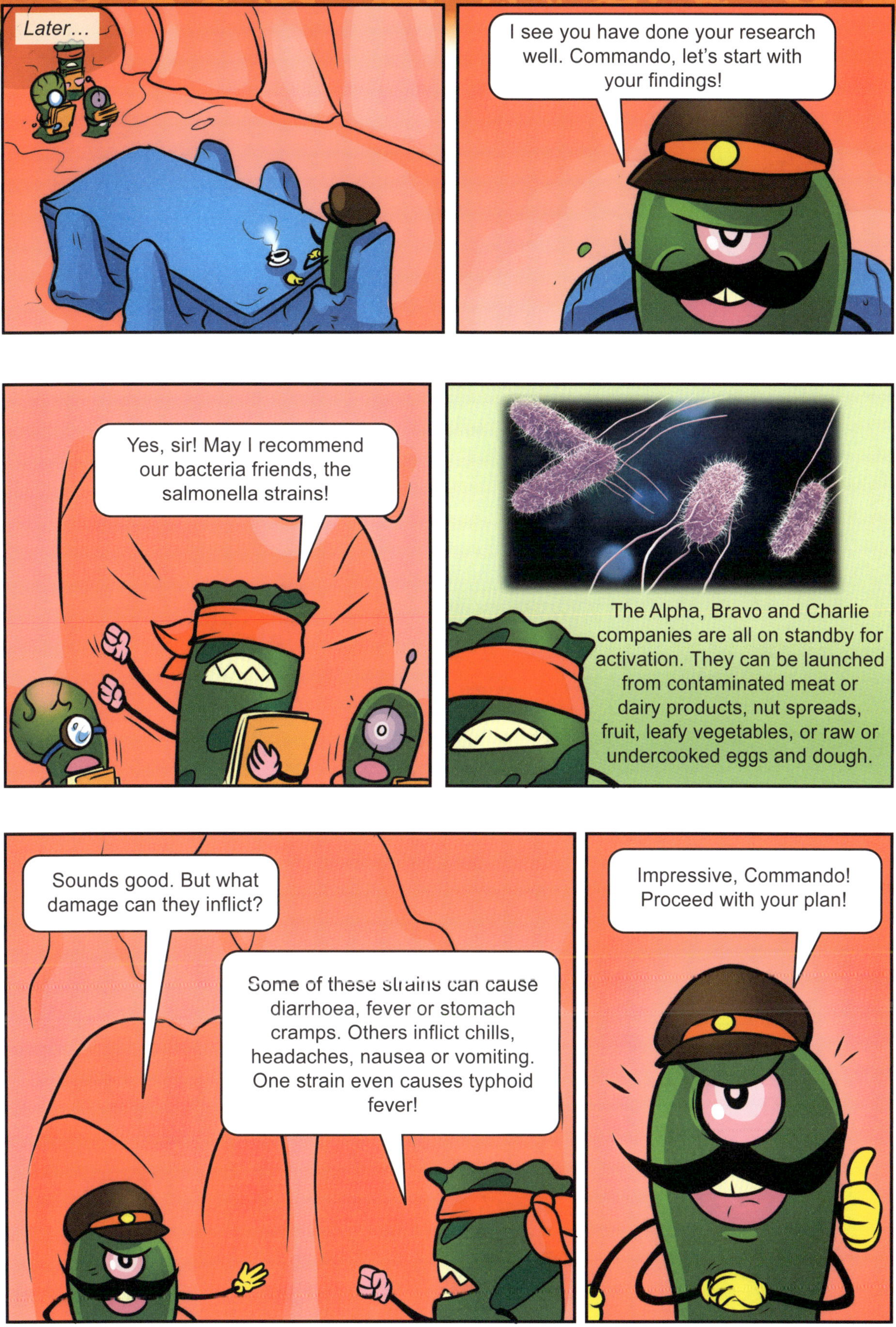
Later…
I see you have done your research well. Commando, let's start with your findings!
Yes, sir! May I recommend our bacteria friends, the salmonella strains!
The Alpha, Bravo and Charlie companies are all on standby for activation. They can be launched from contaminated meat or dairy products, nut spreads, fruit, leafy vegetables, or raw or undercooked eggs and dough.
Sounds good. But what damage can they inflict?
Some of these strains can cause diarrhoea, fever or stomach cramps. Others inflict chills, headaches, nausea or vomiting. One strain even causes typhoid fever!
Impressive, Commando! Proceed with your plan!

I will speak next, sir!
Let me unveil our secret agent… a type of bacteria called *Vibrio parahaemolyticus*!
A complicated name is always a good start. Tell me more.
People in this country love seafood, so that is where I propose we attack. The *Vibrio parahaemolyticus* bacterium loves sneaking into raw or undercooked shellfish, especially oysters.
Yes, I have seen these humans stuffing themselves with shellfish and raw oysters! Good research, Sniper.
Thank you, sir. Damage-wise, *Vibrio parahaemolyticus* is just as deadly as salmonella, if not more! It can cause infection if released into open wounds. This infection can trigger chain reactions in the body, causing organ failure that may even result in death!
Very impressive, Sniper. Please proceed!

Intelligence Officer, this whole brilliant plan was yours. What do you have for us?
Thank you, sir. I give you our most versatile weapon, norovirus! Like the bacterial agents introduced earlier, norovirus causes diarrhoea and vomiting.
Diarrhoea and vomiting are starting to sound like old news. Tell me: how is norovirus versatile?
Well, norovirus is not restricted to seafood. It can contaminate just about any kind of food. It can even be spread from utensils used for eating. Infected people can also transmit the virus directly to others.
That's fantastic! We can hit anyone who eats – and that means everyone!
Well done, team. Now go execute these exciting plans!

What Is Food Poisoning?

Food poisoning occurs when we consume food that is contaminated by one or more of the following:

- ***microorganisms such as bacteria, viruses, fungi, parasites or algae.***
- ***harmful chemicals such as insecticides, fuels or cleaning products.***
- ***natural toxins such as those found in poisonous mushrooms or puffer fish.***

Here are some common symptoms of food poisoning.

- *Diarrhoea*
- *Vomiting*
- *Nausea*
- *Stomachache*

When a harmful or irritating substance enters the digestive system, the body tries to expel the substance by vomiting or having diarrhoea.

Treatment
Most cases of food poisoning last 2–5 days and can be treated at home. It is important to drink lots of water to replace fluids lost through diarrhoea or vomiting.

Professional Help
If symptoms persist for more than 5 days, a doctor should be consulted. If there is blood in the diarrhoea, high fever or failure to retain fluids, consider being admitted to a hospital.

Prevention
Eat only food that is thoroughly washed and cooked. Wash your hands often, especially when preparing food and before eating.

Teething Problems

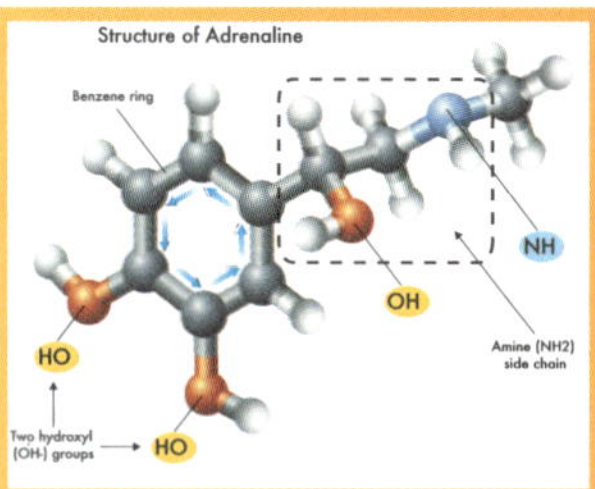

High on Adrenaline

Adrenaline is a stress hormone, a chemical produced by our bodies in preparation for a thrilling or challenging situation. Adrenaline increases the heart rate and directs blood to the muscles, boosting energy. But having high adrenaline levels over a prolonged period can damage the blood vessels, increase blood pressure and raise the risk of a stroke or heart attack.

Dental Health

Mouth bacteria feeds on sugar from the foods we consume, producing acid that damages our teeth. Holes in tooth enamel are called cavities, or tooth decay. You can prevent tooth decay by eating a healthy diet, drinking plenty of water instead of sugary drinks, and brushing and flossing your teeth regularly.

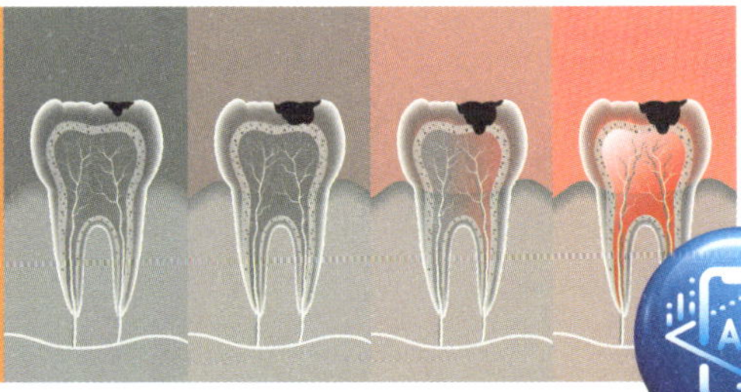

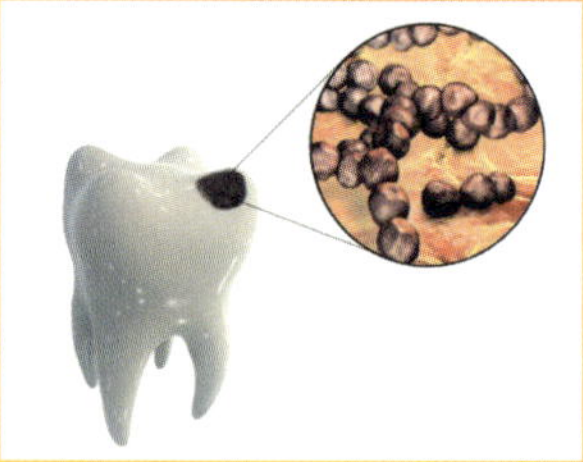

Bacteria in the Mouth

Bacteria lives all over your mouth. *Streptococcus mutans* is the bacterium responsible for tooth decay. Other kinds of bacteria, such as *Treponema denticola* and *Porphyromonas gingivalis*, cause inflammation of the gums.

Good Dental Habits

It is hard for your toothbrush to reach the spaces between your teeth, so it is very important to floss in addition to brushing teeth. Flossing helps remove food particles and prevent the build-up of dental plaque, a sticky film of bacteria that forms on tooth surfaces. Adding a mouthwash to your dental routine also controls the growth of mouth bacteria.

Trigeminal Connection

The trigeminal nerve is a large nerve in your head that sends touch, movement and pain signals from your face to your brain. Experts believe that pain from a tooth infection can irritate the nerve and trigger migraine, a type of headache that can cause nausea or vomiting. Clenching the jaw, head or neck muscles can also cause a tension headache.

Eye Cannot See

Oh noooo!!!!
Arrrggghhhh!
Alert… Alert! We've lost one pilot. Avoid the eyelashes at all costs!
Uh oh!

Code red… Code red! Another germ is down, taken out by the eyelid.
Grrr… he forgot his training! Hold positions, and wait for the eyelid to reopen.
Are you okay, Mike?
Yes, I think so. Some dust got blown into my eyes just now.
Successful infiltration… I repeat, successful infiltration.

We are locked in position and waiting for the target to make his move!
STOP!!!
Don't you remember? Mum said rubbing our eyes was a sure way to spread germs in them!
But my eye itches. I think some dirt must have got in.

Try blinking. It will activate your tears to help wash the dirt particles away.
Thanks! It feels better, but… still a little itchy.
Yes, you do seem to have a speck of dirt in there…
I know! Eyedrops!

Aaaarrrggghhhh... mission failed!
Hey, it worked, I can see everything clearly now, and the itch is gone!
That's great! Remember the right way to deal with dirt in the eyes next time. No rubbing!
Ha ha! There won't be a next time!

Conjunctivitis and Our Eye Defence System

Conjunctivitis is a common condition that causes redness or inflammation of the conjunctiva, the thin layer of tissue covering the eyeball. Conjunctivitis is sometimes referred to as "red eye".

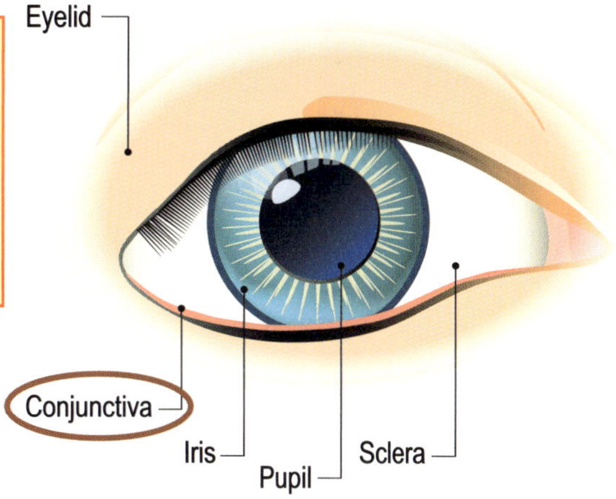

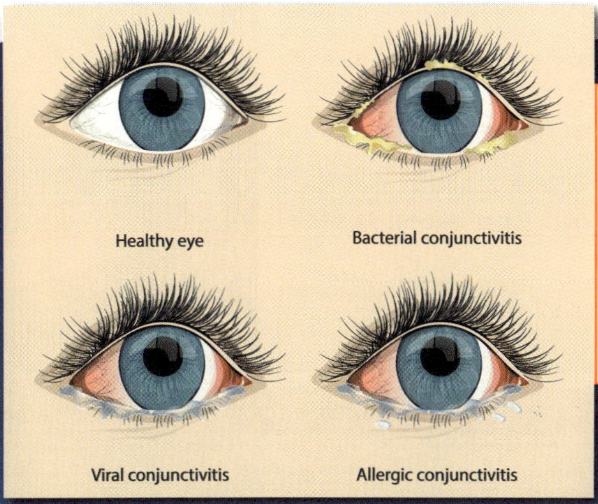

Conjunctivitis can be caused by a viral or bacterial infection, or by an allergic reaction. Viral conjunctivitis is usually caused by touching the eye with hands contaminated by an infectious virus. That is why we should avoid rubbing our eyes with our hands.

The protective mechanisms in our eyes include:

- *eyelashes, which shield the eyes from dirt or dust particles.*
- *eyelids, which cover the eyes and protect them from dust and dirt. Blinking the eyelids also spreads a layer of tear fluid over the eyes, for added protection.*
- *lacrimal glands, which produce tears to keep the surfaces of our eyes moist and clean. Tears also contain substances that attack pathogens and protect the eyes from infection.*

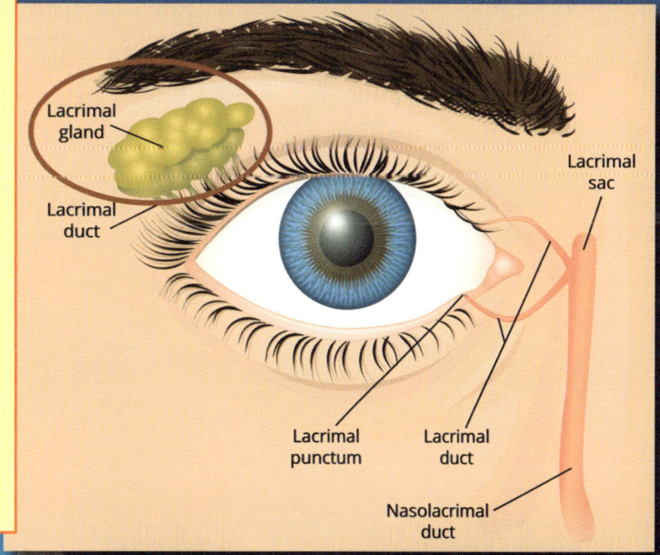

So, How Much Do You Really Know About Germs and Your Health?

Challenge yourself to recall key moments of your Adventures with Germs and Your Health, and find out where you rank on the Health Scale!

Get ready, get set, scan!

HEALTH SCALE	
10	Professor of Microbiology! Congratulations, we're impressed!
9–8	Germ Expert! Good gut instincts!
7–6	Microbial Scholar! Take a closer look!
5–4	Rookie Researcher! Run those tests again!
3–0	Lab Assistant! Read your notes again!

Where do germs live?
Why is plastic waste harmful?
Which animals have winter coats?
What is the darkest known material?
How do barcodes work?

Introducing the sensational new ***World of Science*** comics series designed specially for inquiring young minds! Experience Science come alive through dynamic, full-colour comics enriched by Augmented Reality.

Books in this series so far:

- ***Birds***
- ***Plants and Fungi***
- ***Insects***
- ***Aquatic Creatures***
- ***Human Body***
- ***Land Animals***
- ***Reptiles and Amphibians***
- ***Natural Wonders***
- ***How Things Work***
- ***Great Minds***
- ***Germs and Your Health***
- ***Green Movement***
- ***More Land Animals***
- ***Materials***
- ***Technology and Gadgets***

Look out for ***Endangered Animals, Useful Plants and Fungi, More Materials, More Natural Wonders, Discoveries and Inventions,*** and many more!

To receive updates about children's titles from WS Education, go to **https://www.worldscientific.com/page/newsletter/subscribe**, choose "**Education**", click on "**Children's Books**" and key in your email address. Follow us @worldscientificedu on Instagram and @World Scientific Education on YouTube for our latest releases, videos and promotions.